Earth Angel: My Life's Journey

~In Dedication to God~

***"DON'T TELL GOD HOW BIG YOUR PROBLEM IS;
TELL YOUR PROBLEM HOW BIG GOD IS."***

Published by Krystal Lee Enterprises (KLE Publishing) Copyright © 2025 by N L Hodge.

All rights reserved. Please send comments and questions:
KLE Publishing
770-240-0089 Ext. 1
sales@KLEPub.com

To Reach the Author: N L Hodge
Email: ilovemenh@gmail.com

Printed in the United States of America.
All rights reserved. No part of this book may be reproduced or transmitted in any form or by any means, electronic or mechanical, including photocopying, recording, or any information storage and retrieval system without written permission of the publisher except for brief quotations used in reviews, written specifically for inclusion in a newspaper, blog, magazine, or academic paper.

ISBN: 978-1-945066-74-0

Table of Contents:

1. Breaking The Cycle Pg. 4-5

2. How My Upbringing Influenced My Unhealthy Habits Pg. 6-9

3. The Intoxicating Cycle of Addiction Pg. 10-10

4. Intimate Partnerships & Encounters with the Justice System Pg. 11-13

5. Adjusting to Motherhood & Becoming Responsible Pg. 14-16

6. Rekindling my Relationship with Alcohol Pg. 17-23

7. The Beginning of a New Friendship, the End of My Relationship & Entering the Dating Scene Pg. 24-27

8. Misery Loves Company: My Introduction to Hard Drugs Pg. 28-30

9. Entering & Exiting the Cycle of Abuse & Addiction Pg. 31-45

10. Moving, Shifting & Trying to Overcome Toxic Cycles Pg. 46-53

11. Overriding Self-Limiting Beliefs & Shifting the Narrative of my Life Pg. 54-57

12. On the Cusp of a Breakthrough While Battling Setbacks Pg. 58-64

13. Slipping into Prescription Addiction & Spiraling Towards a Spiritual Awakening Pg. 65-83

Once I started my spiritual journey, I decided I wanted to help change the world. This book will speak to many different people from all walks of life, and it is my true story. This is just the start of me changing the world. We are all here on assignments and we all have our parts to play. All it takes is a belief and anyone can achieve their dreams. Don't let negative circumstances or people change your beliefs. No matter who or what you believe in, always assure to first and foremost believe in yourself. Be kind, compassionate and express gratitude authentically. Surround yourself with like-minded kindred spirits and watch your life transform for the better, to a higher degree than you could have ever imagined.

Remain positive!

I love you all....

Breaking The Cycle

Thanksgiving, age 47, is a day I will never dare forget. It was a pivotal turning point in my life, essentially etched in my memory bank as my fate date. It was a day that I pre-emptively feared yet came to appreciate in hindsight. For the last seven years, I'd been addicted to pain pills but on this fateful day, the addiction was broken. Sure, there were "other bad days". However, this day, this day was the day! Instead of securing a new prescription of pain pills, I decided to substitute all herbal supplements as a replacement, and it was one of the best decisions I have ever made.

The first herbal supplements I got weren't the best, but they did ultimately lead me in the right direction. Dealing with the void of refraining from ingesting any prescription substances, I did not feel like myself. I was in no mood to go anywhere, I had no desire to get dressed, I had no appetite, I didn't want to see anyone but when I took my herbal supplements my day ended up turning around for the better. Whenever I felt as though I was on a downward spiral, I would take another supplement to really push through the remainder of day. I wanted to really figure out an effective regimen that would keep me balanced as I transitioned out of my addiction.

Now, I have tried this herbal supplement many times over and it never quite worked the way it did on this day. On this day, the herbal supplement worked for me a great deal. Now on the day after Thanksgiving, I did relapse and ingest two pain pills. However, something was noticeably different. An undeniable inner knowing revealed to me that I didn't even really desire the pills per se. What I truly needed was energy and most importantly to combat feeling unwell. The following day I argued with my fiancé, urging him to go to the store and secure another herbal supplement for me.

I had a habit of taking pills early in the morning right after I woke up, so I treated intaking this herbal supplement the same way. My finance is someone who pays attention to things that are healthy and otherwise good for the body, so he thoroughly read through the description section of several herbal supplement products until he found the best one for me. I would eventually fall in love with the effectiveness of this herbal supplement, and it would ultimately change the trajectory of my life.

Once I took the herbal supplement my fiancé picked out, I couldn't believe how fast it worked and how good it made me feel. At that point, I made the executive decision to officially replace my prescription pain pill habit with an herbal supplement regiment. This is something I visualized, it was something I re-iterated to myself and it was something I consistently spoke to my family about. All in all, I knew for a fact that this was not my final destination.

The universe works mysteriously and unbeknownst to me, I had unconsciously manifested stopping the use of pills. I was led to believe that only 1% of people can stop powerful medications. However, I am here to tell you from personal experience that I am an outlier, I am a part of the 1% and if I can do it you can do it too. Now prescription pain pills weren't my only battle, but it would prove to be a battle that I would ultimately triumph over.

How My Upbringing Influenced My Unhealthy Habits

A cold wintery snowstorm swept through the state of Ohio and welcomed me into the world on a bicentennial year a bicentennial year, on December 1976 to be exact. In the spirit of nostalgia, I believe this is why I adore the winter season and snow so much. I actually appreciate all seasons, but I love the wintertime and the cusp of winter the most, the fall fashion & colors are so warm and enchanting. As a child, I had a great life, complete with; family, support and lots of love. I was spoiled and more often than not I got what I wanted. As far as lineage, I was my mother's first child and my father's third child.

Although my mom and dad split up, my dad and I remained closed, and my mom assured to support me in every aspect of my life for my entire life. My mom was always an independent woman that didn't need a man or anyone she would simply take care of whatever needed to be taken care of. Despite our many differences I acquired this ability from her. However, at our very core, resilience is what we truly have in common.

Without words, my mom displayed how I was to be in this world. Leading by example; she worked hard, stood firm in her beliefs, annoyed the hell out of me but she was always there when I needed her and still is to this day. She was always such a great support system through all the trials and tribulations that I faced growing up.

My mother had great parents which is where I believe she got her strength and endurance from. My grandma who was essentially my "other mother". She was from a small town in Kentucky and relocated to the Midwest which is where I was born and raised. My grandaddy who was my "present dad" was from Georgia and hopped a freight train at the age of 12 which landed him in the Midwest where he would fatefully meet my grandmother, marry and have six children. I don't think it could have gotten any better than the grandparents I had. Their house is a crucial part of all my childhood history. Every holiday, each dinner, and nearly all of my most important events occurred in their home and inevitably with them involved.

These weren't just weekend grandparents, although I give much respect to weekend grandparents, there was a stark difference in how they showed up for me. These were everyday grandparents and for not only me but for all of their grandchildren. I'd like to think I held a special place in their heart and was indeed their favorite based on the fact I was their first female grandchild. I had three cousins who were really like brothers because of how close we were in both relationship and age.

Since there were three boys that preceded me, I grew up following them and ultimately became a tom boy which I wouldn't change for anything in the world. Our childhood was the best, we had everything we wanted and needed growing up, they always protected me and are still very protective of me to this very day.

My grandfather would drink so he always kept a beer nearby. In hindsight, this is where my drinking habit started, at the tender age of 12. It wasn't that my grandfather condoned it, it was indeed my own personal secret. My family didn't know I drank because I had stolen one of my grandfather's beers. After stealing the beer, I descended into the basement and while listening to music I gulped it down all at once. After I ran around my grandparents' house singing and laughing. I threw up multiple times and dizzyingly enough, my head was spinning terribly.

Like everyone who has experienced the unwanted side effects of drunkenness, I said I would never dare drink again. However, little did I know, this was the turning point of me unleashing the hidden beast. I didn't start drinking regularly with immediacy, but I eventually started and once I did, I lived to regret it wholeheartedly.

Because I grew up a tomboy, I felt most comfortable around boys. But I had one female friend from school who introduced me to smoking cigarettes, liked to drink and hang around boys like me, so we grew close. I'd like to think she also introduced me to smoking weed but that was never really my thing although I would smoke when it was around and then regret smoking weed every time because I didn't like how smoking weed slowed me down. Later in life I would return the favor to her by introducing her to cocaine at the age of twenty-six.

Being at my friend's house at such a young age, I got to experience freedom with no rules. I believe I was fascinated by that, and so I would hang at her house most days during the week and all day on weekends. She was very promiscuous, but I couldn't bring myself to be as promiscuous as she was. I think it goes back to my upbringing because I couldn't be as promiscuous as her because her upbringing was anything but normal and the opposite of what I was inclined to do.

My friend and I would also hang out late at night with random men and getting in and out of the cars of strangers. This was very dangerous for us but fortunately we never had any bad experience that threatened our safety or wellbeing. We did, on one occasion, get stranded by two men who were mad because I didn't sleep with him. My friend slept with his friend, but he was the driver and since I didn't sleep with him, they left us.

Everyone always told me I was growing up too fast and that I needed to slow down because I was still so young. I thought I was grown but had no clue what adulthood was really all about. One day I came to my grandparents' house and my uncle, who was there, told me I looked like a prostitute because of all the make-up I was wearing. I stopped wearing make up after that because I was still a tomboy and still liked to wear baggy clothes and gym shoes (sneakers). I didn't start dressing more femininely until I was eighteen years old.

My friend was the youngest of her thirteen siblings and had nieces and nephews who were older than her (the backwards family affect). Her mom gave her up at a young age. Her mom was a raging alcoholic, and my friend never knew her father. She had so much trauma and pain she didn't realize, as a child, so she would go on to ultimately do the same with her seven living children. She had a total of nine children but two of them passed away.

The Intoxicating Cycle of Addiction

Drinking, which I loved to do, would always get me in trouble, lead to encounters I would regret, didn't remember or both, and years of people telling me what I did while under the influence. I ended up in jail, not for anything major, but for doing things while intoxicated like getting three DUIs, disturbing the peace, and busting out two of my ex's car windows. Later, I keyed my daughter father's car, but no police were involved. I was also put out of clubs, maced and getting myself into fights despite the fact I hated fighting when I was sober.

Countless random encounters with men, losing jobs from being too hungover and calling off work too much. This led me to drink more because I was too embarrassed to face all the things I'd done while under the influence. I would just drink more and continue to make more embarrassing moments and disappointments to myself and loved ones. It was like a never-ending loop and a slippery slope because this led me to drink more and more.

I really don't think I had any dreams early on because it was at the point that I only looked forward to drinking and partying. I did get my GED and some college degrees later. Drinking and drugging was something that followed me for twenty-nine years. I always remained professional when I was working and I had good jobs at a young age, I just always seemed to sabotage them all due to my bad habits.

Intimate Partnerships & Encounters with the Justice System

At just 13 years of age, I found myself losing my virginity to a boy I had my first crush on. It was only a one-time thing because he wasn't really feeling me like I felt him, and he was also what we called a "player" a guy who had multiple girls. I was also considered "young" and unlike these days' boys wanted older versus younger girls. I would then have a flame with another boy and become pregnant at the age of 14, which ended up in abortion, which I still regret to this day.

The guy who impregnated me was eighteen years of age and technically I was a minor, so it makes sense how he didn't want anyone to know we messed around, particularly my oldest cousin. My oldest cousin was the most overprotective of me, well known and respected in our neighborhood. One night, while at the apartment the guy I was impregnated pregnant by someone started knocking on his front and back door simultaneously. He acted like he didn't want to answer so I convinced him to, and this was about to get worse than anything I'd ever seen before.

He was a small guy so when he answered the back door, the guy forced his way in and then opened the front door for the other guy who was knocking. They looked like older men, and I ran in his bedroom but then they brought him in there at gun point and didn't even address me, so I quickly ran out. I couldn't believe it, couldn't have been professionals because professionals don't leave witnesses, and I saw everything.

I only lived around the corner but on the walk home I was so shaken up, I didn't know what to do. Once I got home, in a panic I told my mother and boyfriend what happened, and they suggested I call the police to his house which I did. He called me shortly after, now safe but robbed and told me I should not have called the police and that's when I understood the reason why and how he earned his money. When people make money illegally, they don't call the police because then the police would wonder what they are doing to cause them to get robbed.

14 years of age was another memorable age but not in a good way as this would be the age I would be introduced to juvenile, probation and the court of law. Reason's being, running away, cutting school and fighting my mom. I had become out of control, and this went on for over a year, straight. At this age I didn't care, I actually thought it was cool. Through it all, my mother still hung in there with me, while many girls like me, mothers had turned their backs on them.

After this, I meant a guy who would become my brother for life. We both loved to drink and skip school and back then that's all you had to have in common to become close to someone. We went for years like this and then we wouldn't speak for a while and then we would reunite. He would ultimately become a quadriplegic, for nineteen years until he would finally succumb to his injuries. He was a ladies' man and was shot at close range, by a small caliber .22 pistol, over one of his ladies. It was so hard to see him in that condition and I used that as an excuse to stay away. We would, however, talk on the phone all the time for hours.

I was finally 15 years of age, pregnant again and this time I kept my child, which would become one of the best decisions I made. Having her slowed me down and caused me to get on the right track. Her dad was my first love but due to my drinking and promiscuity he didn't believe my child was his and acted accordingly. He would drink but not as much as me and he was a drug dealer so we were always hanging at dope houses and riding around in cars of people who would trade their cars for drugs.

There was another guy from our neighborhood, which I slept with a few times, when my daughter's father and I broke up, which was often, and the guy told my daughter's father my child was his child. This guy was also known around our neighborhood as a lunatic and a lot of people feared him including my daughter's father so once he told him that, it caused a permanent strain on my daughter's father and I relationship.

All the girls from the neighborhood, were teenagers, and all pregnant at the same time. We were all pregnant by the guys from the neighborhood. Everyone knew each other and some cheated with friends on both ends, friends of the girls and of the guys. One of my girlfriends, from the neighborhood and I were both pregnant when we stole a car from a guy we knew. The guy we stole a car from was a drug dealer and was traded the car for drugs by the owner of the car's son while the owner was away on vacation.

Because of my encounters with the law, I knew technically the son, who rented the car out for drugs could not report the car stolen so my girl friend and I kept the car for four days and drove it as if it were our car. I can't remember how we got the owner's contact information, but we did and when we knew they were back from vacation, we made an anonymous call to them letting them know where the car was parked so they could retrieve it.

Adjusting to Motherhood

The time had come for my child to be born, and I was now 16 years of age. I was alone and gave birth to my daughter with only the hospital staff and of course God. It wasn't all bad, I just don't think people took the situation as seriously as it was, and I don't regret any of this experience. It was part of my strength. Having a child alone at just 16 years of age gave me a sense of responsibility and I learned a lot from it. I would often read my books during my pregnancy, my doctor had given me, on everything about labor, delivery and parenting so I was well prepared.

Having a child at this young age was as equally interesting as it was a pleasure. For the first time in my life, I wasn't only responsible for myself, but I also was responsible for this tiny, innocent human being and the love and joy of being a parent felt great. She was also well advanced, in every way, and well loved and taken care of by myself, and my family. Everyone loved her, wanted to see her and proud of her; she was always in high demand as she still is now at the age of thirty-one.

When my daughter was only six months old, her father went to prison and didn't come home until she was fourteen years of age. I went on to meet her stepdad who I would be with for eight years and he raised her as if she were his biological child. He didn't have any other children so for him, it was as though he'd had his first child too. It's rare that men step up and assume this role, but he did, and he was great at it. When her father was finally released from prison, they grew very close and spent a lot of time catching up, but her stepdad refused to let his time and memories of raising her be taken away from him, even if it was by her biological father, so he remained in her life.

Despite it all, at 16 years of age I went on to become a good mother, except for the night of the biggest party in my neighborhood where I got pissy drunk literally and figuratively (due to not being fully healed and unable to hold my bladder following the recent birth of my child) and my friends and I couldn't get a ride home because I had urinated on myself. I was so embarrassed, and it would be the talk of our neighborhood for a long time.

Following the incident of me urinating on myself, I decided to stay away from the people in my neighborhood and focused on raising my child as a single mother, so I got my first real job and my first car. I never thought about high school, prom or anything that had to do with school because I'd stopped going to school in junior high which had been replaced by my going to juvenile detention centers. I had initially started school one year early but then I was held back, so they never knew what grade to put me in, so they put in slow learning classes. Not because I had a learning disability but because I have a behavioral problem.

I did go on, at 17 years of age and took GED classes and ultimately received my GED. It felt great, I got it the year I would have graduated, so I didn't waste any time and for the first time it felt like I had things together. Although I was now drinking alcohol daily, the worst days were still to come.

I also experienced the joy of having my daughter's first birthday and birthday party, and this is around the time I met her stepdad who I would be with for the next eight years. He was my first adult love; I loved my daughter's father when we were together, but we were only kids. Her stepdad and I were grown, not legally, but we both had responsibilities and would be together well over legal age.

Rekindling my Relationship with Alcohol

Although the required age to enter a bar was twenty-one, at 18 years of age, I had my first experience with entering a bar and was hooked from there. I also had my first car wreck leaving this same bar at 19 years of age and it really was my fault because I was drunk. What saved me was because I left the scene running about a mile and a half, home, and turned myself in to the police the next day when I was sober.

What saved me from being charged with leaving the scene of a car accident was because multiple witnesses saw the guy acting aggressive and irate when I hit his car. He was stopped in the middle of the street talking to someone when I flew into the back of him. He was cited because legally, a person can't stop in the middle of street for any reason other than traffic and he was stopped just to talk to someone. If I wasn't drunk the natural thing, I would have done was just go around him. I dodged a DUI that night, but my car was a total loss. However, no one was hurt.

By the time I was 20 years of age, I met a lot of new people who I connected with over drinking alcohol and partying. Friends I'd grown up with, who didn't party, I found myself drifting away from and gravitating to those who liked to drink alcohol and party. Not all my friends, I grew away from just the ones who didn't like to drink alcohol or party. Out of all these new people only a few became actual lifelong friends. We did, however, have a lot of good and bad times and created a lot of good and bad memories as well.

My 20's came and went so fast mainly because I was drinking alcohol and partying so much. I have vague stories only because someone else had told me. The first part of my 20's, I was still in love and my boyfriend and I, were always together when we weren't working. Although he and I liked drinking alcohol and partying it was only me that it would affect causing him to be one of the people who would tell me what I'd done while drunk. I would eventually sabotage our relationship because of my actions while being drunk and, at times, caused him to stay away. It was never his choice, only his reaction to my actions.

I took him through so much and he kept trying to be with me. A time of two when we broke up, he would remain in my daughter's life. My daughter and family loved him, and our families grew close. His mother was my hairstylist so when he and I separated, she would know and so I would go elsewhere to get my hair done during our separations. I would always cause our separations, not him, and we didn't separate often.

Through my family, I was introduced to what we called "get togethers" at my aunt's house where there was plenty of food, alcohol, fun, love in and a great time. Everyone was welcome. It was always a safe and positive environment to which I would usually get drunk and pass out. On one occasion, I passed out at my aunt's house in her bed and when I woke up, I was still drunk from the night before and had to use the restroom, but I couldn't find my pants in time. My kid cousin's coat was the only thing I could quickly grab so I wrapped it around me and walked through her house to the restroom. We still laugh at that memory today.

Although it wasn't one of my drunk bad memories it is among one of my drunk funny memories. In my aunt's younger age, she would always have these get-togethers, but I was only a kid, but my childhood memories would be of them doing the exact same thing as I ended up growing up and doing. Even as a kid it was always a great time. Listening to music, dancing and playing cards is still a tradition of my family and my family still gathers at my aunt's house on holidays and special occasions. A lot of days it didn't have to be an occasion; we would all just gather at her house and enjoy each other's company.

I ended up getting my first DUI and I was still underage because the legal drinking age was twenty-one. I was leaving an after-hours place which is where we could continue to drink alcohol and party even after the bars closed at two a.m. I was by myself when I decided to go get something to eat. The last thing I remember, it was dark out, my music was blasting, and I was near the menu to place my order for food.

I was awakened by the police, who had tapped my car window outside my car. The music was still blasting; I had fallen asleep, at the menu, after placing my food order. I was arrested but not taken to jail and had to call my mother to come get me. The police parked my car in a safe parking place until I could get sober and return to get it. My mother was very upset but like always she came to get me and pretty much fussed at me all the way home.

Although I was now 21 years of age and legal, nothing really changed because I had been living as an adult or at least acting like an adult since I was 16 years of age. I had a child, I was drinking, smoking cigarettes and weed, I had a car, job, boyfriends and was sexually active. I was more of an adult than some actual adults. It still felt great to have the actual identification that proved I was 21 years of age, and I loved to show my identification off.

One day, I was leaving home to go to work, and my car was gone. It had been repossessed by a title loan company who I had not paid because of my excessive drinking alcohol and partying. I had heard of repossession but really didn't know much about them. When I told my mom what had happened, she told me I could file bankruptcy and get my car back. She was right. I filed bankruptcy and got my car back; however, it would later become another total loss for me, but I didn't have any insurance and could not afford to get my car fixed, so I was without a vehicle for a second time.

I felt stuck not having a car. I couldn't go out to bars as much and it was hard getting back and forth to work so I knew I had to get another car as soon as possible. I eventually got another car, and I loved a certain make and model, so I would always get that same kind of car. Back-to-back I had two vehicles stolen, which I ended up getting back shortly after both times. One night it was freezing outside so I ran into the gas station to get cigarettes and left my car running. The teenagers jumped in and took off.

The second time my car was stolen, I visited a friend who was in town and went to his hotel room. I assumed it was valet parking, although I didn't see a valet attendant and I left my keys in the ignition of my car while I went to my friend's hotel room. When I came out about an hour later, I looked all over but my car was gone and when I asked the hotel staff, they informed me there was no valet parking. Both times I had left the keys in my car.

At 22 years of age, my drinking was still very present, but I was enjoying life, working, in love and spending time with and raising my daughter. My boyfriend and I mostly rode around the city while drinking alcohol, smoking weed and listening to music, which was as fun as it was dangerous. Fortunately for us, we didn't have any negative situations as a result, at least, not from anything that came with drinking and driving but I would get drunk and start arguments with him. We also had great times too, not every time it resulted in me starting arguments, especially if I was smoking weed because weed calmed me down.

It was vacation time for both of us, so we decided to go away for the weekend to our state fair which was about a two-hour drive to the capital city of our state. I ended up getting very intoxicated that night although we had a great day and enjoyed the fair, but this night, I drank liquor which made me behave way worse. I was normally a beer drinker, and beer could get me drunk but liquor got me extremely drunk and turned me into someone completely different in a bad way.

It would be almost if I was possessed by the devil because I would become the total opposite of myself, make ALL bad choices and decisions and flip out on anyone I was around. I would not remember the next day and would have to be told what I had done the night before while intoxicated. People couldn't enjoy themselves around me when I was drunk because they would to take my car keys, watch me and make sure I made it home safely. For a while I didn't see a problem with my behavior.

Once my boyfriend and I started to drink that night, I became upset over a song and that's what set the argument off. I was petty. I said and did a lot of hurtful things to him that night so the next day, now sober, I still act as though I was right even though I knew I wasn't. That became a normal technique over the years of my drinking, me just acting as if I were right and defending what I had done wrong when really, I was embarrassed and just too afraid to admit it. I would eventually apologize often using the excuse "I was drunk".

Having this immature attitude and approach, I ended up riding all the way back home in the back seat which was ridiculous and that was probably one of our first experiences of many, with me behaving this way. He was so forgiving; I did so much wrong to him, which I regret, be we remained together, and I apologized but still would do the same kind of things. This also wouldn't be the only time we traveled on what was supposed to be a nice vacation, resulting in me ruining the whole trip by being drunk.

With me being a young lady, I still wanted to be older because there were still some things I could not do at 23 like getting a credit card, renting a car and even getting into some nightclubs that were age twenty-five and up required. This was the 90s it's not like this today because now being younger is the "it" thing but when I was younger, being older was the "it" thing. Older people seemed to have figured it out or at least that's what I thought, whereas younger people were considered to be kids and kids weren't cool.

Next vacation, my boyfriend and I decided to go to a major city for the weekend and I loved it until the end. Yet again my drinking had ruined the trip. We had a great time visiting friends from back home that had that had moved away. I started drinking alcohol early in the day which I normally wouldn't start drinking until the evening, but I was on vacation, so I drank earlier than usual. Later that evening, I decided I wanted to still hang out but my boyfriend wanted to go back to the hotel so I tricked him in to give me the car keys so I could go to the car where the cooler was. I ended up taking the car and going to a club.

Once I got back, he was pissed but I was too drunk to even comprehend and the fact I drove and made it back safe was by the grace of God. We argued and went to sleep. The next day he got up and we argued again, and he left for about two hours. Me being proactive, I had already assumed he left me so now I was going to have to figure out how to get back home. I called the front desk of the hotel and asked for a shuttle to greyhound. Shortly after calling the front desk, there was a knock at the door. I assumed it to be the shuttle service, but it was my boyfriend coming back to get me and I was so relieved.

We quickly made up I gave him the usual "I'm sorry I was drunk" story, which was the story I would often tell people after one of my drunken nights until people were fed up and no longer wanted to be around me if I was going to be drinking alcohol. I would often tell myself and others, I wasn't going to drink too much but I always ended up drinking too much. My boyfriend and I then proceeded back home, and everything was good until it wasn't, again.

The Beginning of a New Friendship the End of My Relationship and Entering the Dating Scene

At 24 years of age, I was working for a company in which I met a lifelong best friend who remains close to this day and although we hadn't spoken for years, when we came back in touch, it was as if we hadn't missed a day in between. We had what we called a "spot" for every night of the week which was basically a place to go hang out and drink alcohol seven days a week. We had a lot of great times despite my heavy drinking. I introduced her to drinking alcohol, she normally didn't drink until she and I started hanging together.

I was still in a relationship but by now it had become somewhat distant and the honeymoon phase and the days of us spending all our time together were over. In fact, this was the age when I decided to step out on him for the first time by cheating with another man. I would do things like stay out all night with another man and then come home the next day with his name tattooed on me so he wouldn't be upset. I knew I was wrong. He wasn't really into asking me too many questions and making a big deal about things but I'm sure he knew what I was doing.

My new friend and I had many wild and fun nights which still are some of my greatest memories we have today. We both have huge senses of humor, so we were always laughing and joking. We ended up starting the job at the same time and getting fired a week apart for the same reasons; calling off too many times because of our partying every night of the week. We didn't seem to be too concerned so we continued to party as always despite being recently unemployed.

By this time, my relationship with my boyfriend had taken its course and by now I had cheated on him with multiple different men, so I decided to move out from his place, where I was staying and get my own place. What really triggered me was I had run back into a boyfriend from when I was a teenager, and I thought by getting my own place; we could finally be together again. The only problem with that was he ended up going to jail for four years, before it could happen, and the opportunity was missed.

I had been telling him I was planning on moving out and going to look at places, but I don't think he took me seriously. The night before I moved out, he finally expressed concern about why I was moving out and I told him we would still be together and live separately but that wasn't what I wanted. I wanted to be single. Shortly after I moved out, we tried to make it work but that was very short lived; like one night short lived. We never said the words that our relationship was over, we just drifted apart and that was the end of it.

The day I moved in I was in a brief fling with a guy to which I was his senior. Prior to that I never messed around with guys younger than me. It was brief and fun until one night he stayed over and after he left, I noticed he had stolen money from my purse. Turns out that's how he made his money by stealing from people and would meet his fate shortly after by being gunned down in broad daylight. They never found his killer or maybe never really tried because some people, not me, were relieved he was killed.

There was another guy I knew as a childhood friend, and we had affairs over the course of years but later in life he too met his fate the same exact way two miles from my previous fling. By this time, death was normal amongst people I knew and had grown up with, but I never liked it, and I never liked funerals. It wasn't because they were hurtful but mostly because they were nerve wrecking. People judging, not liking and hurting others only to show up to their funeral as if they cared. They would show up just to be nosy, gossip and enjoy the festivities that took place following the funeral service.

The age of 25, a great time to be alive! This is where, for the first time in my life, I had an affair with a man who had a woman. The love was real, at least on my end. We'd knew each other as kids but he wasn't really my type; what I considered to be a nerdy skateboard type, and I typically liked men who made lots of fast money and drove nice cars. He had nice cars and this is what drew me to him. We spent a lot of time together, but it was very short lived.

On one occasion, I was travelling to the same major city I had traveled to with my ex-boyfriend but this time with some work friends and I lied and told him I had an abortion with our child, for him to give me the money to travel with. Although the guys I dated drove nice cars and had lots of fast money, they were very stingy and limited in how much money they wanted to give me, cash in hands.

They would pay small bills and spend money on taking me out but wouldn't give me actual cash and if they did give me actual cash, it was given in small amounts. I really didn't care too much because I had always made my own money so anything they would give me would just be extra. I honestly think they had less money than they led on but some of them really knew how to live frugally.

One day we had a simple argument, nothing major, and he walked out. I never saw or heard from him again until twenty-three years later when we connected briefly on social media. Nothing much just catching up, saying hello and that was it. I thought about him all the time during those twenty-three years and often wondered if he ever thought about me over that time. When we connected, I told him that but quickly moved on to another topic because I didn't want to sound like I had been waiting for him all that time. It was nice connecting with him briefly and it brought me closure.

One day when we were out, he pointed out this unique car we spotted which was owned by the guy who painted his nice cars. Because I was hurt after our splitting up and being the vengeful person I was at the time, I saw this guy out while intoxicated and he ended up coming to my house that same night. We slept together that same night, but I don't remember much because I was so drunk. We ended up dating a short while longer until he got on my bad side by denying coming over to my house one night.

I didn't know at the time, but he ended up telling me the reason he didn't come over was because he had gotten a DUI coming from a night club. This would be the second man in life, I became irate with and busted out the windows on his car – even the sunroof. I was so drunk; I called the police on myself and was arrested. That ended things for us and once again I sabotaged a relationship by excessive drinking and bad decisions I made as a result.

I was still always drinking and smoking cigarettes and even though I would meet a guy, I really felt like it was only a matter of time I would do something in a drunken state and sabotage the relationship and I did every time without failure. It was almost as if I manifested these results. I never felt worthy and often I would think about getting back with my ex-boyfriend, but I still didn't really want that no matter how bad my luck with men and relationships were.

Misery Loves Company: My Introduction to Hard Drugs

After more drinking, countless encounters with men – some I can't even remember, at age 26 I would be introduced to cocaine. Like my aunt who had the get-togethers, I would have the same atmosphere at my place so it was a hang out for our generation. Cousins, childhood friends and occasionally random people. I would go on to get everyone around me hooked on cocaine like I was, not sure if it was from a misery love company perspective, but more so I just told people, and they would make the choice to want to try and eventually become hooked.

At this point, my place only attracted coke heads, and I didn't care who knew I used cocaine once my mother found out, but others cared about who found out about their cocaine usage and wanted to keep it hidden. We were like vampires, up all night and slept all day. I even messed around with a few guys, because they were cocaine dealers, and I could get it free. Some of the dealers I liked but a couple were not my type. Even still, I messed with them and didn't worry too much about it.

By this time, I was addicted to cocaine plus alcohol and if I thought my alcohol days were something, it would not compare to my cocaine plus alcohol days. I ended up losing my job, which was totally my fault and could have been avoided twenty-six times because that's the number of days it finally took them to fire me; no call no show 26 days in a row. Most jobs only give a person two chances but this job, which was a great job, gave me twenty-six chances. I was a great employee just had an issue with attendance.

Jobless, addicted to cocaine and alcohol, no money and it was getting to the point no good men wanted me. I had lost so much weight, I wasn't taking care of my hair, which was something I cherished by getting my hair done every week, but now I simply didn't care, I was too hooked on cocaine. I even slept with my landlord to avoid having to pay my rent, but he wasn't buying it he slept with me and still evicted me. He was police officer and owned the building in which I was living.

One night I was lying in bed in the darkness and suddenly saw lights flashing outside my bedroom window. I heard a beeping noise and had already known what it was, so I didn't even get up to witness my second car being repossessed. The next morning, I looked out my bedroom window and my car was gone. I was losing everything I had worked so hard for, but it was all because of my drinking alcohol and daily cocaine usage. These were the causes of all my financial problems ever.

This time I couldn't file a bankruptcy to get my car back because the law requires it be seven years from a previous filing and it hadn't been seven years. My mother wanted to help me because the jobs I would get would require a car due to their distance from where I lived. She cosigned for me to get another vehicle which would ultimately get repossessed, resulting in me not only hurting my credit but her credit as well. She was disappointed but not too upset.

Since I was now being evicted, I was lucky enough to find another place before I was put out. Everyone gathered at my house the night before and we partied all night. We all slept through what we had planned for moving out time. The next day everyone had to be back at work, so another friend of mines helped me move the following day, but it was much harder because it was just me and him. My mother hated my bad habits and choices, and she was very vocal about it almost daily.

My daughter was staying with my mother even though she had a bedroom at my place. It was best she stayed with my mom because I was unfit at the time and would make excuses about it being because of her school's location, to feel better about myself. In all actuality, her school was closer to me. I was still in my daughter's life, not as much as I should have been, but I always had full custody of her. She was always my greatest joy, and I loved her so much, but I was young when I had her and really didn't know how to be a great mother.

Entering & Exiting the Cycle of Abuse & Addiction

    At 27 years of age, I finally met a man who I would be with over the next twelve years. We were set up as a blind date by a friend of mines who was dating one of his friends. What brought us close and allowed our relationship to grow was the fact we had the same bad habits. He wasn't really my type, and I would not have dated him if it weren't for our commonalities. I ended up falling in love with him and for the first time in a long time it felt good having a man I was in love with and enjoyed until he showed his dark side.

    People normally leave someone for things such as abuse, infidelity, betrayal and financial reasons and he would commit each one of these with me. One moment things would be going well but as soon as he sniffed some cocaine, he would flip out on me and beat on me. Countless black eyes, busted lips, broken nose, broken ribs and now I was pregnant for the third time with my second child. He knew my child was his, but he would get hi and ask "is that my child" then one thing would lead to the next and now he's a crazy mad man.

    What I would think were some of the best days would ultimately lead to worse days full of fear, uncertainty and pain. Not just physical pain but emotional pain as well. I would always forgive him when he sobered up and of course he said he wouldn't do it again at least a hundred more times. I was familiar with people forgiving me for flipping out when I was under the influence, so I felt it was only right to forgive him, and I thought I loved him so much but really it was just convenience.

He was shockingly a great dad, when he announced to his family, "We were pregnant, people who knew him would tell him make sure he didn't hurt the baby. I finally asked him why people said that repeatedly and he told me his ex was pregnant with their child, and he ended up fighting her causing her to miscarry. That made me scared, but I was hopeful he wouldn't hurt our child, and he didn't although on one occasion I thought he did. I would hear the joy in his voice and see the look in his eyes of how happy he was to be expecting a child.

Coincidentally he was from the same major city I traveled to in the past with my ex-boyfriend and coworkers and eventually I would go on to relocate to that same city by way of mismanaging money due to my bad habits and losing everything once again. I was too ashamed and too embarrassed to stay in my hometown and moving away would become one of the best decisions I ever made even though I didn't realize it at the time.

I was now 28 years of age, and this was probably my worse year at the time. I was pregnant, miserable, still being abused and hurt. I also worked full time almost up until the delivery of my child. I wish I could say this was as easy pregnancy, but it was not. It was, however, loving and nurturing from my end to my child. Although all these things were happening in my life, I still found serenity from within. I couldn't see myself with another child and often wondered how it would be once my son was born.

I was still partying while I was pregnant, but I still managed to make all doctor appointments, eat right and take my prenatal vitamins every day. The partying and bad habits, however, were still there. One day my child's father picked me up from work and we were both arrested and taken to jail. We both ended up getting the charges dropped but the process was horrible. I had to spend my whole paycheck to get out and then borrow money to get him out.

At 29 years of age and just twenty days later, it was time to have my child. My son's father and I headed to the hospital at five in the morning because my doctor had scheduled the delivery. Coincidentally, the same doctor delivered both of my children thirteen years apart, so I was familiar and comfortable with his delivery methods. Neither one of my labors was super painful, but I would still tell them I could feel pain so they could give me more medication to decrease the pain. It was a numbing sensation so I could not feel myself push during delivery and the doctor had to use forceps both times.

I was so uncertain of how things would be when my child came but it was surprisingly good. All the pain, fighting and bad habits were still there but everyone around managed to love my child and there was definitely a strong support system. This gave me a sense of peace because for all nine months, I had thought about this regularly. It seemed like my child's father was waiting for me to have the baby so he could start fighting me and one night, shortly after giving birth, I went off and broke a lamp over his head defending myself from him.

There was blood everywhere, he had to get both stitches and staples, and I finally felt like I defended myself and he now knew what I was capable of and therefore would not put his hands on my again. I was wrong, however, because the following time we fought, I called the police, and he took off with my child in my mother's car she'd been letting me drive back and forth to work. Given the nature of the crime, I am surprised they didn't issue and amber alert but I knew how much he loved his child so I wasn't worried about him hurting him, but I was worried about where they could be. He ended up returning soon after and, like always, I forgave him.

A few months later I ended up losing my job, which was another great job, and this is when I decided to move away and start fresh. My family was always close, so they didn't like the fact I was moving far away, in a tumultuous relationship with a small child. I also had to make the decision to leave my first-born child who was now thirteen years of age. I felt like I was stuck in between a rock and a hard place because she was thriving in school, a part of a basketball team and had close relationships with her friends. She would, however, relocate to live with me in the coming years and has become a huge success in life.

Once relocated, I hit the ground running, while trying to get on my feet. At first, we stayed with my son's father's family, who welcomed us and what I thought to be was a kind gesture was anything but. They were supportive, regarding our son but that was it. This would, however, become one of my favorite persons – once we moved out. I was so home sick and wasn't used to living in such a big city, so a lot of things were different. I had to learn about this new place, and I could not understand a lot but ultimately ended up loving it.

I was 30 years of age when we finally found a place and moved out and things were good for a while. My son's father ended up fighting causing visible injuries. Once I escaped from him, I went to his family's house and when she saw my face, she called the police right away. That caused him to have a felony warrant out for his arrest, and it was going to be a rough road ahead for us both. Once I healed and we made up, I didn't want him to go to jail but he did and now I was in a big unfamiliar city, didn't know many people and with a small child.

I was so home sick, and I missed my family so much and they were even trying to encourage me to come back home, but I couldn't because I was too afraid of what people would think and say about me. A large portion of my life was built on this principle. I always cared too much about what people thought of me, and it affected many of my decisions in my young adult life. Despite my feelings I ended up staying. I was always resilient, but this called for a different deeper kind of resilience and that led me to know I could do anything by the grace of God.

I ended up helping with getting his charges dropped. Due to the event of him fighting me and taking my mother's car and my child, the police agency in my hometown put a TPO out on him against me. The reason why his case was so serious was because of that. Not the fact he fought me, and my face was all bruised. It was because he did it, under what they thought, was an outstanding TPO so he was charged with aggravated stalking which is very serious. The strict laws in this new city were among some of the things I had to learn quickly.

Once I found out this information after several weeks of calling many, many courts and law officials, I ended up getting a letter that the TPO had been dropped prior to the date he fought me, so the detective submitted it to the court for a reduced charge and after four months he had time served. It was great to have him back to help me with our child, but our worst days were still to come. The fighting didn't start up right away after he was released, this time, but there were still more hurtful days ahead.

While he was locked up, I was hanging out with this girl he introduced me too prior. At first, I thought she was cool, but she was a smile in your face and stabbed you in the back type of woman. We connected because she and I were alike in that despite our bad habits, we still had good jobs and took care of our business. One night she and I were hanging out when I discovered his boxers and that's when it all made sense, this is where he went after the time, he fought me before he was arrested and jailed.

Once I discovered his boxers at her home, I was so upset, I went down to visit him at the jail and banged on the glass so hard, I was put out of the jail. I had a super temper both under the influence and/or sober. Up until that point, I had heard of people being put in jail but not put out a jail. This would also be the beginning of discoveries of how this new city operated legally. Laws in this new city were much stricter than the laws from back home.

After that, I got evicted, so I had to move back with his family for a short period. I had to move by myself with one box on my hip and my child on the other because I lived up so many steps that I didn't want to leave my son by himself that high up. I was working at this time, so it didn't take long for me to move into my next place. The partying and bad habits were still very present, but things were probably the best yet between my son's father and I.

By 31 years of age, the partying and bad habits were still there but I was working the best job I'd ever had so money was plentiful, and I felt like I had things in order, for the first time in a long time. I believe it was easter weekend when he broke my ribs, and I went to the doctor with my child and the nurses had to watch him because I was alone, and he wasn't allowed in the examination rooms with me.
That was so embarrassing, and the hospital staff were pressuring me to press charges, but I lied and told them I already had. I had to provide a case number, so I used the one from when he was in jail.

He traveled for work so after that fight, he left and the next day coming from work my car died and I was told I had sugar in my gas tank. He swore up and down it wasn't him and even tried to put it on a family member I accused him of having an affair with, but if that were true and that family member really put sugar in my gas tank, then that only confirmed my accusation of them having an affair. I thought about this for a long time.

My oldest cousin, who was really like a brother, decided to relocate and stay with us for a while and we continued to party, but the fighting had stopped due to my cousin being around. The fighting was still there, just not as intense. We had some good times, and he was a chef, so he often cooked for us or brought food home from a restaurant in which he was employed. He was good with my son and my son liked having him around. He was always good with my daughter too when she was younger, and he would babysit while I worked.

My cousin would end up hooking up with the same girl I found my son's father boxers at, she was easy, and although he didn't really like her, she really liked him. She provided my cousin with a place to stay, party and unwind rather than him always being around us. I think she was in love with him, but it was hard to tell because she would always say things while being drunk and hi and then say something different when she was sober. She was also and very bad liar. I learned all about liars due to the people I had come across from my past.

Fortunately, I was never really in any dangerous situation, besides the ones provoked by my son's father, but I knew people who were and heard many stories. Out of all the dangerous people in the world, the most dangerous person, to me, was the man I had a child with and slept next to every night. One night we got into just an argument and the next day while I was at work, he moved the bedroom suite out of our place, from which he had bought for us.

He hated my ambition and the fact that, no matter what, he couldn't stop or control me. Once I got home and saw what he'd done, I went right to a furniture store and bought a brand-new bedroom set and he was speechless. He begged me to take it back, so he could bring the one he'd taken back, but I didn't because that would have just been something he would do every time he got mad at me and. He would start arguments with me accusing me of cheating when all alone he was the one cheating on me.

At 32 years of age, I knew we were going to end up being evicted again, due to partying and mismanaging finances. I had two new cars, one brand new, and the other used new. I couldn't afford the payment for both and allowed my cousin's longtime friend who happened to now live in this new city, to take over the car payments. That was short lived, and I ended up having to retake possession of the vehicle. I still couldn't afford both vehicles after that, so I surrendered it back to the financing company. Even though I gave the car back, it was still considered a repossession so technically I had a fourth repossession of a vehicle. My third repossession took place when I lost everything resulting in my relocation to this new city.

We moved to our nicest place, yet, but the partying was still there. Our son was now in daycare so rather than my son's father being a stay-at-home dad, he was now able to do whatever he wanted while I was at work, which wasn't often since I missed work each week and only showed up when I wasn't under the influence or hung over. I could never work under the influence; if I was drinking and getting hi there was no way I could work, I felt like those festivities were time to party.

The fighting, between myself and my son's father, had improved and wasn't as intense but they were still very present and often. He would get hi and accuse me of cheating and then get sober and swear he would never do it again. By this time, we had been together for four out of twelve years. I still loved him and kept hoping he would get better since now it wasn't as bad as it had been in the prior years. His infidelity was also still present, but it also was not as bad as it had been.

He would never admit his infidelities, but I would always find text messages and pictures in his phone. On one occasion, I went back home to visit and when I got back, I discovered naked pictures that weren't selfies; someone had taken the naked pictures of him. The pictures were taken in the home we shared so that meant he had someone in our place, while I was gone and if he was naked, I'm sure they had sex. As usual he had some lame excuse. I can't even remember the excuse he used but I do remember it was a bullshit excuse, and I knew what I knew.

My second oldest cousin had come to visit for the weekend, so they went out to a strip club and my son's father came back with glitter all over his face which means he and the stripper got a little too acquainted. That resulted in an argument once he came home. The next day, I went to get in my car and found he had gone into my car and broke the handle that controls the blinking signals. Lucky for me, the car was a brand-new car, and still under warranty and the dealer replaced the part for free.

One night we were sitting and watching TV when he announced he had been on heroin and warned me if I see him getting sick, it would be because he was going cold turkey. I knew what heroin was but had never been around anyone on it, at least not that I know of, but I had experience with taking pain pills when I could get them. My pain pill consumptions were far and few between so I wasn't familiar with withdrawals or any side effects with them, but little did I know, heroin would be an ongoing battle for him.

We used to keep a plate in our kitchen cabinet, so my son could not get access, and one night I sniffed what I thought was cocaine, but I knew I didn't have the stimulating cocaine vibe. I was, too calm, and relaxed and this led me to believe it was heroin. I'm not sure if he left it there knowing I would use that place next time I was using cocaine, or if it were an accident. It was hard to tell with him because he could be as sweet as he was conniving.

His excuse was that he had a friend over and the friend used the plate to break down and sniff a pain pill. He lied so much about anything, so I never knew what to believe but we quickly moved passed it and continued to party like always. From that experience, I stopped using plates for cocaine and started using right out of the pack by breaking it down and using a straw instead. This way I didn't have to worry about accidentally consuming something I had no knowledge of. Although using drugs is a risk within itself, I still used cautiously and safely.

Using drugs took a lot of time, energy and money. We would ride across town to get drugs and then have to break it down, roll a dollar of find and cut a straw and make sure we were careful not to spill it. It took way too much effort but that's what we enjoyed doing at the time. There were also times when plates would fall or someone would spill their drink on the plate, thereby ruining the cocaine which was a waste of money. Sometimes it would even be our last money.

My 33rd birthday came, and my friend came into town. She and I were going to the Bahamas the next day, so we went out. The club we went out to had male strippers on one side and female strippers on the other side and because I was the birthday girl I ended getting a dance with a male stripper. I noticed I couldn't find my son's father and went on the other side to find him and there he was cozied up in a corner with a female stripper.

I was livid because here it was my birthday and our last night together until I left, and he was up enjoying the company of another woman. I was humiliated in front of my friend and when we got home, we argued and fought. I ended up going to the Bahamas with a black eye. All I could think was that he'd done that on purpose he always seemed to be a little jealous of my success and the fact I was going to the Bahamas is what this was really all about. Although it was embarrassing, I still went to the Bahamas and had a great time.

My friend and I would travel often and no matter where we went, I would manage to find cocaine, so I did the same in the Bahamas. She was one of my few friends that didn't use cocaine. The next day in the Bahamas we were on a beach and started day drinking Bahama Mamas. The bartender then ended up just giving us the whole bottle of liquor where I drank most of it. We met a nice lady who was there with her mate who was employed on a local cruise ship, so she hung on the beach and drank with us.

She was from the same county we were from but lived across the country from where I lived but we would keep in touch for a while via text. She told me once she got back on the cruise ship, she was so drunk they had to put her in a wheelchair which I thought was so funny because we were both so drunk. The friend I went with would drink but never get drunk so she would watch me and make sure I was ok. This became a regular thing between us; her watching out for me when we hung out.

I ended up finding some cocaine from a guy on the beach which was dangerous but by the grace of God I would always find the right thing and it was good every time. The guy ended up having another friend, so we all decided to hang out together. Later that night, it was carnival which is an event where island's party in the streets and everything is a big festival.

While we were having a great time at carnival, I met a guy, who looked like he was a big deal. Women were swarming around him, and I could tell he was a big deal in his country. Because I was so drunk I can't quite remember how we met but I ended up sitting with him in his car, where he'd been playing loud music and was being idolized, so I felt excited knowing he'd chosen me to sit with him. What I later realized was that he only had one arm. I was a loud drunk so once I realized he only had one arm, I confronted him about it.

That didn't end very well so the guys we were with took us back to our hotel where I removed my sunglasses, and they saw my black eye. They went through the whole spill about how the person that had done this was a coward, I was too pretty to accept this kind of behavior from anyone, all the stuff I would hear because of being with this abusive person. I would always try to defend him, knowing it wasn't right. People thought I was stupid and told me he would never stop which he never did.

The next day it was time to return home and because I was so drunk the night before, I almost overslept thereby missing the opportunity to shower and change clothes. I brushed my teeth and washed my face, and we headed to the airport. It wasn't until we got back to our country that I realized I still had a bag of cocaine and a cut straw in my jeans pockets I was wearing. Just a thought of how boarding an airplane with an illegal drug could have gone terribly wrong scares me to this day. We landed back home safe and sound.

Life was back to normal, and my son's father and I ended up moving to a bigger place in the same area as our current place. He would sell tickets at major events like concerts and sporting events and would often come home with something for me or my son. Following one of the events he'd worked selling tickets, he came home with a turtle who I still have. I never knew turtles lived as long, or possibly longer, than some humans. Turtie is our turtle's name, and he would go on to travel with us and move across states with us over the coming years.

Now at the age of 34, the fighting between my son's father and I started to escalate again. He ended up with another warrant because he called my family, back home and told them he was going to kill me. By this time, I was fed up, scared for my life and decided to take my son and relocate to a new city. I didn't want to move back home but I wanted to be close, so I moved to a neighboring state to my hometown. I don't think he really believed me when I told him we were moving but he quickly realized I was serious.

I got pregnant three times almost back-to-back, but I didn't want to bring another child into the toxic environment. I had already had one child who had seen and been through a lot with his father and me. It's as though he wanted me to keep having his children, but he was so unpredictable and when we would drink and use cocaine, he would act crazy. We never fought when we were sober, and he was a good man when he was sober. He was mentally, emotionally, verbally and physically abusive when he wasn't sober. No more children needed to be around him, or me, if I was going to continue to be around him. I was pregnant a total of seven times with two living children.

Because he was a great dad and I never wanted to keep him out of his child's life, I allowed him to help me pack and move. My oldest cousin came to help and had planned to drive the U-Haul back, but we ended up partying the night before and once again, I missed the move. My mom had rented the U-Haul for me, and it had to be back, so my cousin had to leave with all my belongings already packed in the U-Haul and drive back by himself.

The following day, my son's father and I ended up heading to my hometown which is where my belongings were and everything turned out fine. He kept telling everyone "We" were moving but only I had planned on moving. There was a lapse in dates in which I could move to my new place so I stayed with my mother for a week and went to the other city to put my things in storage. I continued working at the same job because I was able to work from home.

I would end up working for this company for fifteen years and it was my best job yet. I was often awarded top performer, highly successful and respected working by management and coworkers. I loved it, it was great money and what I considered to be easy work. I started working for the company when there were only five employees, including myself, and it would become a multimillion-dollar organization with over fifty employees and countless clients.

They put up with so much from me, excessively calling off and tardiness, but I was making money for them more than most of the employees who showed up every day on time. I loved it, I loved the people I worked with, and I loved the support everyone gave to one another. This was my first time having a job with these kinds of personalities. I always had great jobs, but this one was by far the best. I also worked closely with upper management which I hadn't in any previous jobs.

Moving, Shifting & Trying to Overcome Toxic Cycles

It was finally time to move to my new place and many of my childhood friends and family came along to help. I had another friend from my childhood, and she had been living in this new city, so she introduced me to some of her neighbors. She and I were tight and always stayed in touch and while she liked to drink, she did not like the cocaine. Since I was open about my habit, I told her, and this is what her neighbors and I would have in common.

She didn't like the fact that I would hang with her neighbors without her, but I continued to tell her it was only because of the bad habits we had in common. Her neighbors were also troublemakers, they would go back and tell her I said things I really didn't and vice versa. She and I ended up not speaking for a while as a result, but I kept hanging out with her neighbors. Mainly because one of her neighbors was a dealer so he would always have cocaine both using and selling.

While she and I weren't speaking, one of her neighbor's girlfriends, told me her son was killed. My heart dropped. This was the third time in life she and I would be mourning and grieving over someone close to her who passed away. First it was her son's father, then her brother, countless friends and now her son. Her son! She was devastated and despite the fact we were not speaking, I had to go to her. I will never forget that day.

She and I would become close again, but she would always find reasons to not want to speak to me. She let too many negative thoughts get the best of her. Falling out with me about things that weren't even true. Meanwhile I would try my best to befriend her and she only gave in when it was convenient for her. This last time she did this, I decided I would love her from afar and no longer wanted to continue this up and down friendship.

Many of my family members decided to come to visit me since I was now living closer. The night before they arrived, I was up all night getting hi and drunk so when they arrived the next day, I was already drunk. My family loved to drink alcohol but not the drugs so I wouldn't indulge around them, at least not in their face. Instead, I would act as if I had to go to the restroom and partake there before returning. Like the days of my younger years, we all still had a great time. We were packed in like sardines, but I wouldn't have had it any other way.

Before they came, I made sure to get everything I knew they would like and want so we had plenty of good food, plenty of alcohol to drink and a fresh desk of cards since we all loved to play cards. We didn't even go anywhere, and everyone was fine with that because we enjoyed each other's company so much and this was the first time in a long time we had all been together. Today we still talk about how much fun we had when they came to visit me.

Although I worked from home and was making good money, I would still blow my money on partying so one day I came outside to get in my car, and it was gone. It had been repossessed for lack of payments even though I had the car for five years and had paid almost double what the car was worth. I ended up filing my second bankruptcy, to get another vehicle. Over the years and despite the good money I made I always had poor credit due to my poor spending habits and because of my constant partying with drugs, alcohol and smoking cigarettes.

At that time, the law stated a person could get a vehicle even before the bankruptcy had been discharged but there were only a few car dealerships that would honor that law and the cars they sold would look good but be in horrible condition, mechanically. Because of this, I found myself having to pay to fix something on the car every other week because I needed my car, and paying to have it repaired was my only option. The car was one I would have never purchased if my credit and finances were better, but I was just happy to have a car, and it got me where I needed to go.

At age 34, I decided to give my son's father another chance because I didn't like being alone with just my son. He moved in for a while but one night we were getting hi had a fight and he left stealing my car, so he would end up in jail in this new city. Alone again and with him in jail, I decided to move into a townhouse across the street from where I was living. It was on the same property, in fact, when the movers got there, they didn't bother to put my belongings on a truck, they decided to walk them across the street.

Once again, I had to learn the laws of a new city because of my son's father's habitual experience with the court of law pretty much all over the country. He is the only person I know who has been in jail in so many different cities and states. Because he traveled selling tickets, he was always on the road, resulting in many arrests, many hard aches and wasted money. The DA put a TPO on him against me when he was arrested, and they told me if he contacted me, they would know, and they sure did.

Seventeen charges were filed on him for violating the TPO because that's the number of times he'd called me from jail after they told us to have zero communication. When someone calls from jail, there is a recording that states "this call will be recorded and monitored" and while I never gave it any though, it was very true. The DA told me about our conversations verbatim. I didn't want to press charges, so he spent a few months locked up because of the calls but not for stealing my car or assaulting me which is what he was originally charged with.

What I didn't know about were all the warrants he had in other states so when it was time for him to get out, he was extradited to another state to face the charges. This went on over two years and four states when he was finally released. These were only the felonies; he had a dozen misdemeanors across many other states as well. Lucky for him, they don't extradite for misdemeanors otherwise that time frame would have exceeded more than two years and included more than just four states.

While he was locked up, I decided to go back to the state I had just previously moved from to see his family and some friends I had made. One of the friends I made was a girl, who ended up being my neighbor from the previous state I'd moved from, but I met her after I moved. I met her because her and my son's father were having an affair when we stayed at our last place in the prior state. She had been calling his phone, which I had, because he was in jail. She was a drinker and liked to use cocaine like me.

Once she and I talked, my heart was broken knowing how he was accusing me of cheating when he was the one cheating all along. She and I would continue to talk on the phone, and I kept pretending she was my friend but deep down I was still hurt. She was another person who we would only call each other if we were drunk or hi. That was pretty much my relationship with anyone I was close with during this time in my life. I'd planned a visit to go back to my former city, since my son now had family there and I told her when I would be coming. She and I planned on getting together once I got into town and we did.

By this time, I was 35 years of age and had arrived where she and I got together and hung out with my cousin's friend who had already lived there for a while now; the same one I allowed to take over car payments when I lived there. Everything started out good until it wasn't resulting in me going into a drunken/hi tantrum about how hurt I really was. I just couldn't hold it any longer and once the alcohol and drugs kicked in, I let her and everybody that was around, know how I felt. I just wanted her to know it was not okay to sleep with your neighbor's man and then act like everything was good.

I was also hurt by that situation plus everything he had taken me through all coming to surface through my emotions. My cousin's friend liked me or at least pretended to like me, so he was flirting with me that night. That would become a random affair he and I would start to have over the next few years. It was nothing on a regular basis but rather very random when one of us was in the same city or state. I knew my cousin would not like this, so I never told him. I'm sure he eventually found out or at least had an idea. At first, I thought my cousin was overprotective because I was young, but his over protection would be a lifelong thing.

After that, I apologized to her for my behavior which is what I always did when I would sober up, so we remained in touch. I later found out she and my cousin's friend, who I introduced to her, and were trying to flirt with me, had started a relationship causing her to fall in love with him. This showed me it wasn't a one-time thing with her having an affair with my son's father, but now she was in a relationship with my cousin's friend knowing he liked me. She and the same girl my cousin dated while he was living with me, was much alike, scandalous; they also shared the same zodiac sign.

I ended up getting a DUI while I was there visiting and was arrested. I went to jail and once again, like in the Bahamas, I had cocaine and a straw in my wallet inside of my purse. The police didn't find it nor did the jail, so it was still there when I got out the next day. Once again, I totally embarrassed myself and was happy to leave so I didn't have to face those who knew what had happened. My rental car was towed when I was arrested so I had to get another ride to the airport.

I was relieved to be back home but had to now come up with money for an attorney for my new DUI, so I didn't have to come to every court visit. There were quite a few court appearances before I ultimately had to return to appear before the judge. I was still drinking, drugging and driving as if I didn't already have an ongoing DUI case. Because I got the DUI under my license from the previous state and not the state in which I currently resided, my current license was not suspended and the DUI never showed up on my current license.

I had so many incidents, in which I didn't know how I made it home and oftentimes when I woke up, I would look at my car to make sure it was there and not damaged. One night I ran out of gas on a dark road and my son was with me. The first police pulled up, he came up to my window and saw I was out of gas. I was visibly drunk and wreaked of alcohol. He got my license and went back to his car when the second officer pulled up. Once the second officer pulled up, I just knew I was going to be arrested for DUI.

Once the first officer came back to my car, he gave me my license back and told me because it was such a dark road, he would wait in his car behind me while the second officer went and got gas for my car. I was shocked at how I dodged the bullet of being arrested for DUI and even more shocked at how nicely the officers responded by helping me. Once the second officer returned, he put the gas in my car, and I went home completely amazed. Look at God!

I found myself having to file a second bankruptcy. My expenses had finally gotten the best of my finances, and I was now broke with bad credit again. It was as though I would get back on track, make good money, but would still find myself financially broken. It seemed like I would just wait seven years so that I was able to file another bankruptcy. I always told my mother, but no one really knew just how financially unstable I really was. Although it appeared I was always spending money, what people didn't know was, that was my bill money and bills were left unpaid. It was an illusion.

At 36 years of age, we had a huge snow and ice storm, below zero freezing weather and by now I was over these kind of winters. I grew up in the snow and cold, so I was familiar, but I was also over it, so I decided to move back to the state I had relocated from prior. In this state, they didn't really have winters as cold and nowhere near as much snow. I was excited to move back, and my son's father would conclude his jail tour there so once again we decided to give it another shot. My bosses at work knew I was moving back so I now had to go into the office twice a week and was still allowed to work from home the other days. The commute was 1 ½ hours in the morning and 2 hours in the evening.

My son's father was finally getting ready to be released from jail finally, which just happened to be his home state and the state I was moving back to. When we decided to get back together, he was still in jail so it was convenient for me to move back so we could raise our son together. Of course, he gave me the jail talk about how he was going to do right, and all the negativity was behind us. Those words were shortly lived once he got out. I thought we were going to get married because we communicated about it often while he was in jail and that was one of our plans.

When I moved back it was June, he was released from jail in July and by December, right before Christmas, he was arrested again in another state. This completely ruined our Christmas plans as we were going to go home to see my family; I made sure my son got to spend time with my family each Christmas and summer when school was out. This Christmas and my son's birthday, which falls four days after Christmas, were ruined for us because of his arrest. It was also an inconvenience because I was always the one who had to go to or call these different cities and states I knew nothing about when he got arrested.

I was somewhat familiar with the state he was in jail in but not this county. Cities, states and counties all have different laws and ways of doing things so every time he would be arrested, I would have to learn the laws of wherever he was jailed. Although it gave me a lot and knowledge and insight, it was still stressful at the time. I am grateful for the lessons I learned because that only helped me confirm just how resilient I really was.

Overriding Self-Limiting Beliefs & Shifting the Narrative of my Life

I would often let the facts of my past mistakes, failures, and the use of substances dictate who I was, but deep down I always felt like I was more. I had such inner strength and when people would tell me when I was younger, I paid it no mind. I used to think older people didn't get it and that they didn't know what they were talking about. I must have learned this from negative influences along my journey because I now realize, older people have all the wisdom. I grew up around older people and thought their upbring was different than mines because they were from a different time.

At the time I didn't realize life and history repeats itself and some would say "same game; different players" and that's very true. It's the game of life just played out in different realities. I also later found; "we don't see life as it is, we see life as we are" again very true. This means two people can experience the same situation and both have different opinions depending on their level of awareness and consciousness. Learning these things helped me overcome my past mistakes which allowed me to move forward.

I just recently started to understand this although people would say things like this when I was younger, but I would quickly dismiss without a second thought. Once I did learn, I knew I would change the world even if it only meant sharing my life story with others. I feel as though many people can relate and let them know they are not alone, and they can change whatever they are unhappy with. Not just drugs and alcohol, but anything in life. I've always felt like I was more than just drugs and alcohol and I think that's why I have been so blessed by remaining faithful to God.

I always prayed mostly before I started indulging in substances because I wanted to be in a sober state when praying, and I would pray for my safety and my family. My family, children and I always prayed no matter what. No negative circumstances or situations could take our minds away from praying. I knew for a fact God got me through impossibilities and I've lived so many and still living them. Still praying and believing and now even stronger than ever. I'm grateful for everything I thought at the time, that were bad experiences because I always came out on the other side; victorious.

I would always go back to hometown to visit family and each time, without failure, I would do something under the influence of drugs and alcohol that left me feeling ashamed. My mother would always be disappointed. This didn't happen just a few times; it happened every single time. Some of these actions landed me in jail a couple of times, having my car windows busted out because I was starting fights with people, and I broke my ankle. I would also miss the opportunity to return to my home because I would be too hungover to drive back home. This went on for over ten years.

At the age of 37, I decided to completely end the relationship with my son's father for good. It wasn't because of the fights that had occurred. It was because I was happy thinking we were going on vacation, and he ruined it by getting arrested. He was up to no good while I was with him and led me to believe it was going to be a nice vacation for us. Once again, he was arrested in an unfamiliar place, and I had to drive all the way back home by myself. This was one of the states he previously toured while being extradited but it was a new city and county.

For the last time, his choices had broken my heart. I drove back home in complete silence, once again, embarrassed by him. Once he got arrested, the police found out what motel we were staying at and when I got back to the motel, there were at least ten police cars and countless officers surrounding my room. It was made a big scene and people were watching. I was so embarrassed, but I cooperated by allowing the officers to search the room because I didn't want any trouble for myself. They didn't find anything, but the sheriff told me to never come back to their town again. I couldn't eat or sleep and had to explain the story repeatedly to friends and family. That was the end of our twelve-year relationship. I'd felt there was a reason God kept separating us and I would soon find out why shortly after.

I ended up getting a third DUI following a party at my cousin's house where I had been drinking heavily, and he begged me not to drive but insisted I was okay to drive. I didn't make it for two blocks before I hit another car with my car. The officer couldn't believe the numbers I blew were a 2.8 (over three times the legal limit); my first DUI I blew a 1.7, second DUI I blew a 1.9. This was the highest DUI I'd blown, and they couldn't believe I was still coherent. I didn't remember anything at all the next day, but I still remember how hungover I was.

My son's father ended up spending around six months in jail following our ruined vacation and I kept telling him it was over between us, but I don't think he knew I really meant it. Because I would leave him and get back with him over so many years, he felt as if I would always be there. By the time he got out, I had moved on completely with the love of my life, my current fiancé. The saying 'you get over someone by finding someone else" is very true. Experiencing the love of my fiancé, felt like no other love I had before.

On the Cusp of A Breakthrough While Battling Setbacks

This newfound love ended up being exactly what I needed despite the small things I didn't like about him early on. He was the perfect gentleman and a breath of fresh air from my previous relationship of twelve years. He was smart, handsome and tough. He did like to drink alcohol and smoke weed but he hated cocaine and the fact that I used cocaine, but he saw past that. At first, he would say he didn't want to be in a relationship, but I manifested our relationship, and we are in love more than ever to this very day. Ironically, he was from my hometown, so I knew of him, but he didn't know of me.

We knew a lot of the same people, but he was five years older, so we never hung out at the same places or went to school together. We did, at one time, stay right down the street from one another and even back then I saw how handsome he was. I feel like we met at the perfect time, he was out of a seventeen-year marriage, and I was out of a twelve-year relationship. It never would have worked had we met any sooner. I would always hear stories about him and how tough he was, and I had a liking for bad boys. He possessed everything I wanted in a man.

At first, we would only see each other every weekend, but that quickly moved to several times a week. I just enjoyed being in his company no matter what we were doing, but most of all, I loved talking to him. Despite his "bad boy" reputation, he was kind, gentle, and smart. He knew a lot about a lot and had taught me so much in the short time we were dating. I couldn't stand being away from him and if I wasn't with him or talking to him on the phone, I was thinking about him. He made me feel so good.

Once my son's father got out and saw me experiencing this; he knew it was over. We remained friends and would still sometimes hang out and he was still a good dad to my son. Although he knew I had moved on he still didn't like it. He would still call and harass me for messing with his friends, but I was so head over heels with my new man I paid him no attention. He really believed I was doing these things, to the point he became delusional insisting the lies were true.

I was now 38 years of age when my new man, I'd recently fell in love, called me from jail. He had previously told me he thought there was a warrant for his arrest, but months went by before he would be arrested. During those months it was still a honeymoon phase for us and now we were together almost every day. The day he called me from jail, I thought, "not this again". But it was and now I had to wait eighteen months to be with him again, so I did. I was still drinking and using cocaine, but I slowed down after he and I started dating.

During the time he was in jail, my son's father thought it was finally a chance for us, but it still wasn't. I did spend more time with him, but it was only because he was my son's father and we both liked using cocaine and drinking together. I think I led him on because I would say things while under the influence but really didn't mean them. I did that often and with everyone though. I would always make plans and tell people I was going to do things and then sober up and not even answer their phone calls. This was something I had done for years and had grown accustomed to it.

A buddy from the previous state I was living in called to let me know he was going to be in town. He arrived and like old times we were drinking and using cocaine. Sometimes when I used cocaine, I would stay up all night and because I was drinking the whole time, I would be drunk by day light and then come down and sleep the day away. Even though I would sleep so long, I would still wake up feeling bad because of all the drugs and alcohol and lack of eating.

All that day, I was drinking, arguing via phone with my son's father and he called my mother and told her he was going to kill me. My mother was scared for me because she lived so far away, in my hometown, and knew how volatile he and I's relationship had been. She also told me she thought he was serious because he'd never spoken to her that way despite our years of fighting. So now she was worried, and she had every reason to be.

The following day, when I finally woke up sober, I saw missed calls from everyone in my son's father's family. I knew it had to be serious because he had been to jail so many times before, and they never called me once about it. I was feeling hungover, weak and hungry even though I had no appetite. I would always check my call logs and text messages when I woke up after a day or two of partying just to recollect things I may have done and didn't remember. What came next was already in head but now it was confirmed.

The first call I returned was to my son's father's mother because I knew she would know why the other family members were calling me and I had missed her call as well. I was already crying when she answered and calmly told me my son's father was dead. He had just told everyone he was going to kill me the day before. Even still, I didn't want him dead, and the pain was so severe because I was hurt for myself but more importantly for our son. I knew how much he and his son loved each other.

This would be one of my worse years yet. My car was totaled by a drunk driver on the highway, we almost lost my aunt to a health scare, I broke my ankle, my man was in jail and my son's father was dead. Some of his family and friends were saying his death was my fault because of our tumultuous relationship and he was so stressed. His cause of death was a heart attack, but he was young, fit and ate healthy. Even though he indulged in drugs, he was still very active, and he ate healthier than a lot of people. I later understood why he'd had a heart attack; it was fentanyl related and accidental overdose. His mother knew and didn't tell me, I found out when I finally saw his death certificate a while later.

I'm still not sure if he purposely used fentanyl since I'm told, people who use heroin will use fentanyl because it's stronger, or if it was in the some of the other drugs he consumed unknowingly. I do know one thing; it left me and my son feeling void and now my son had to go through life without his father. When I first told my son, he cried, but he was trying to bury his emotions by staying glued to his tablet. Family is everything because my family all came to visit and grieve with us, which was a temporary distraction, but it felt great having them there with us.

My man called me from jail, and I broke down crying telling him about my son's father passing away. He didn't cry on the phone with me but later told me after we got off the phone he went to his cell and cried. They didn't have a good relationship, but like me, he didn't want him dead. He also felt bad for my son. He was always a great father to his children who were now adults so he couldn't imagine his children having to grow up without him. He also used to tell me how his biological father was never really in his life, but he did have a stepfather who raised him, and that was who he considered to be his father.

I was 39 years of age when my man was finally released from jail, and I was so happy. This was the day I had been waiting for over the last eighteen months. He moved in with me and finally things were going right again in my life.
Unlike a lot of men, all the promises he gave me while incarcerated; were made into reality. Everything he told me he was going to do, he did and more. At the time my son was still grieving his father and even though my man tried to have a relationship with my son, my son wasn't having it.

My son had never seen me with another man; only his father. This experience was different for him, and it took a while, but it finally got there. My son now a young man, kept his father in his heart and wouldn't completely accept the fact of having a stepfather and more importantly, now, living with us but overtime he adjusted. Their relationship would go on to become a rocky road, but we still made it work. My son was devastated at a young age so he's very protective of his heart.

I was just happy things were back on track, and we were living our lives together. My man and I started dating again and doing more things than even before he went to jail, and I was loving every minute of it. He still hated my bad habits, but he learned to deal with them. I was even more successful at work and had gotten several raises by this time, so I was making the best money I ever had. When my son graduated from elementary school, I decided to put him in the marching band in which he started thriving.

Now 40 years of age, my man proposed to me! I gladly accepted and we were now engaged. I planned on getting married in previous relationships but this time it was really going to happen. He gave me a nice ring too. I wasn't in any rush to go out and get married right away but I often thought about the kind of wedding I wanted to have. We had been together and living together for years now so it felt like we were already married. I also wanted to have his child, but we ended up growing too old for that to happen. I didn't want to have a child that late in life due to possible health complications.

I was twenty-nine when I had my son and sixteen when I had my daughter and they were already thirteen years apart, so having another child would have meant starting over for me a third time. It would have also meant, I had three kids by three different men. I don't have a problem with having three different kids with three different fathers, I just never wanted to do it. I don't think anyone does, but it happens and it's all good. I would visualize what our daughter would look like, I was like a little girl in love; my man was my crush.

I only had three crushes in life. The guy who broke my virginity, another guy from my neighborhood but the ultimate was my man and that's who I was with. I was still heavily drinking and drugging and one day my man made me mad and caught me in bed with another man. I was so upset I told him I was going to do it and so I did. I felt so bad afterwards to see how much it'd hurt him. He broke down in tears afterwards when we were discussing it. That broke my heart to see him so hurt and that would NEVER happen again.

He was a faithful man, he never cheated on me or gave me any reason to believe that he was. He would make me mad by hanging out in places I knew weren't good for him. When he did, despite me wanting him not to, I would get mad. I was still immature although I had success and took care of my business. Due to his negative history and "bad boy" reputation, I just wanted him to be safe. The incident of me cheating on him drew us closer together and now I had so much more respect and love for him, and I loved how he loved me.

After that, when he would hang out, I would always be with him. That way I knew exactly what he was doing and when there was trouble, I knew how to get him to leave. There was never any serious trouble, but he had a temper; not against me but with other people. We argued but he never put his hands on me unlike my son's father. This was a refreshing discovery given the history of his nature and the stories I'd heard about him, prior to us meeting. He was very tough and strong and that's one of the many things I loved about him.

I also loved the fact that, as tough as he was, he was just as gentle and sweet. Of course, no one other than myself and his ex-wife and children knew this side of him. He would behave this way with me but as soon as someone else came around, he would toughen up. I had never seen someone transform so quickly but as soon as they would leave, he would be right back to his gentle self. He loved his space and didn't let too many people get too close or know too much about him. He grew up an only child, so he didn't need friends around.

Slipping into Prescription Addiction & Spiraling Towards a Spiritual Awakening

At the tender age of 41 years of age and following me breaking my ankle, I found myself now addicted to pain pills. I could take my pills and feel hi without the hangovers and the fact my man didn't like my cocaine habit, so I traded drinking alcohol and using cocaine for using pain pills all day every day. I thought this was good, for the first time since I was thirteen, I wasn't drinking and since the age of twenty-six I was no longer using cocaine anymore. I heard stories about pills and the fact I would take them here and there over the years, I didn't think they would become a problem plus they were prescribed.

I had no idea what I was getting myself into. This ended up being my worse habit yet, on a different level. I didn't miss my weekends by being high, drunk or sleeping all day but I gained so much weight, and pills became a full time priority. I would only drink alcohol and use cocaine during the evening and if I was using cocaine and drinking during the day, it was a continuation from the night before and lack of sleep. I ended up reconnecting with the girl from my past, where I found my son's father's boxers, and she was getting pain pills prescribed to her too.

She and I would lend and/or trade pills because she got her pills on a certain day, and I got mines on a certain day. I was the driver so sometimes we would ride all over the city to multiple different pharmacies trying to get the prescriptions filled. Due to the pills becoming an epidemic the FDA and DEA had strict guidelines and pharmacies often would not have the high quantities we were being prescribed. I found myself having to have pain pills in the morning before I started work and to be able to function throughout the day. Not necessarily due to pain but because I was addicted.

I would lie to myself and think, at the slightest pain; I would need a pain pill. I would also use that as an excuse when talking to other people in my life. I would always tell myself to make them last until my next prescription, but it never worked and when I didn't have any, I would not get out of my bed unless I was going to get some. Getting pain pills became my number one focus. I couldn't think about anything else until I got some. I couldn't be happy without them; I had completely lost myself.

I tried to hide the fact of just how addicted I was and would often tell people I was okay, and I was taking them as prescribed when really, I would go through ninety, ten milligrams, within three days. They were supposed to last thirty days. I also didn't know about how tolerance increased rapidly with pain pills, but I'd soon find out. Once they were gone, I had to spend time, energy and a lot of money to find more. It was like a job every morning when I woke up. I would always tell myself the night before I wasn't going to get up looking for pills the next day, but it never worked.

I was pretty good at finding pills when I was out of mine, so I never went more than one day without them. I heard the stories of withdraws but just brushed it off as those people are just weak. I was so wrong and was soon going to find out all about withdrawing. One day without pain pills wasn't really bad because, technically, they were still in my system. Two full days, however, was a different story. I was relieved that by now, I was working from home full time and no longer required to go into the office.

Each year, the company I worked for had a big mandatory meeting where all employees had to come in. I had my last dose of pills two nights prior and just figured I would be alright since I would be distracted by our big meeting and not think about pain pills. I always looked forward to these meetings and seeing coworkers I hadn't seen since the year prior and they would make big announcements and give gifts, rewards and awards. There would always be good food and a good time. The night prior to the meeting, I woke up at one a.m. and couldn't go back to sleep.

I didn't realize waking up at the time was just the start of what was about to become, the worst, next few days. Basically, withdrawals are everything you don't want to go wrong with your body, going wrong. I usually loved to eat, but the next day at the company meeting, I discovered I had zero appetite. I also had to excuse myself to the restroom a few times and still didn't realize I had already gone into withdrawal. I couldn't enjoy myself at the meeting I was so ready to leave to see if I could find some pain pills.

Once I left, I still couldn't find any pain pills and things were about to get a lot worse. I got home and just figured I would just go to sleep since I'd been awake since one a.m., and it was now nine p.m. I still could not sleep. I ended up taking something to help me sleep and I ended up falling asleep for a few hours until I was suddenly awakened. I was awakened by the worse stomach pain ever; even worse than both my pregnancy labor's and once I got enough strength to go to the restroom, I was sitting on the toilet and had to grab my restroom's trashcan also. Fluids were coming out both ways simultaneously.

That was the first time in my life experiencing that, people would tell me when they had the flu, they had that experience, but I never had the flu. I was never sick…ever, until I started experiencing pain pills withdrawals. It's something about nighttime with withdrawals because during the day I wouldn't have this experience but at night I did. I would still feel bad during the day, but the sickness came at night. When it happened, I told myself, after this I am not using pain pills again but that would only last ten days and really because I just couldn't find any during that time.

Over the next few days, I couldn't eat, sleep, or enjoy anything and my mind was foggy. My cognitive functions were nonexistent, and I had no energy whatsoever. I didn't want anyone to see me or see anyone and I had the shakes. I avoided phone calls and had my fiancé run all my errands and take care of home. I was grateful I had someone like him while going through this but even he couldn't understand it. I just told my son I was sick, so he just wished me well and didn't pay too much attention to it. He would eventually find out but not at this time, and my daughter was busy with her businesses, so I didn't see much of her. We communicated often but it was via text.

Now 42 years of age and fully addicted to pain pills my life completely revolved around me getting pain pills. Bills that were previously a priority had to now be put on the back burner if it meant me not having enough money to get some pain pills. I also started to distant myself from friends and family. I would look at videos on you tube of people telling their stories of how they stopped, and I would try my best to stop but I just couldn't. I spent thousands on alternative supplements, but nothing ever worked. There were some things that would stop withdrawals when I didn't have any pain pills, but nothing compared to the feeling they gave me, and I was chasing that feeling.

My man really didn't know how bad I was feeling but he soon found out and he hated it. He saw all the money I had been blowing and found out the bills were unpaid and that kept us arguing. On the other hand, he didn't want to see me suffer so he would still help me find or buy some when I didn't have any. I still had my job and made good money; the problems only came when I didn't have any pills. I felt like I needed pain pills to function, and I really did thrive when I had them.

The problem was, I couldn't do anything or go anywhere for long periods of time because withdrawals can start anywhere from six to twelve hours after last usage. I would plan to travel around the times I got my new prescription, so I didn't get anywhere and have to be without pills. I kept trying to trick myself into getting off of them, but it still never worked. No matter would I did, at the time, pain pills were like breathing air for me, a complete necessity.

I always loved shopping, getting my hair done and eating out but for the most part, that all stopped. I still did these things, but they were now far and few between because all my money went to pain pills and bills. It took a while before I was completely bankrupt because I was still making good money, so I maintained my habit for a while - years. Getting pain pills made me happy and while people get excited about their dreams, goals and aspirations, I got excited about getting more pain pills.

When I had pills and money to get pills, I never thought about stopping. I would only think about stopping when I couldn't get any and didn't have any. There would be times when I would have money but still could not get pills but instead of spending the money on anything else, I would hold on to it in case I found someone selling pills. This was extremely dangerous and considering how my son's father passed away, I was playing Russian roulette with my life. I knew this but kept telling myself I was okay.

My 43rd birthday was just another day for me. I would always celebrate my birthday and even look forward to it but by now if I had pills, I didn't care what day it was. It was now at that point, I didn't feel like myself without pills. This was a whole different feeling from the typical withdrawals I'd grown accustomed to. I stopped wearing clothes and I had a lot of nice clothes, and I was now always wearing a scarf on my head when I left the house. I worked from home so I was used to wearing house clothes but now I would wear house clothes even when I went outside.

The pandemic came and all I could think about was the stimulus checks they were giving out because then I would have more money for pills. I still made good money, but it was split between pills and bills only – nothing extra. The thing about pills is the more money you have the more you spend on pills until it's all spent. The higher your tolerance the more you need, the more they cost and the worser the withdrawal. It was a never-ending cycle of cravings and withdrawals.

I'd reach a point where I was no longer getting high and simply taking the pills for energy and to prevent withdrawals. This too cycle would go on for another few years. I would get my tolerance down and then it would go back up again. This was another cycle that went on for years. The lower the intake, the lower the tolerance the less severe the withdrawals would be and the easier it would be to completely stop. This process is called tapering which doctors advise so their patients don't just stop abruptly.

I ended up taking short term disability for mental reasons and this is when I would be introduced to benzodiazepines which also became a bad habit over the next few years. So now I'm taking pain pills and benzodiazepines which were deadly combinations. The withdrawals from benzodiazepines were worse than the pain pills and could cause seizures, although, I never experienced any seizures. I also miraculously, never overdose on either medication even though at time I would take enough to kill an elephant.

Sometimes I would simultaneously experience withdrawals from both. I really felt out of my mind. When I had pills, I would feel normal but when I didn't, I was now paranoid, sick in every way and had a loss of cognitive functions. I felt horrible because now I had to figure out how to get off both kinds of pills. I went to a methadone clinic, but the doctor couldn't help me because he couldn't give me anything to help due to the benzodiazepines and it takes months to taper off benzodiazepines. I now felt stuck, and I couldn't tell my doctors because that would risk them stop prescribing them to me and they weren't MAT doctors.

MAT doctors known as Medication-Assisted treatment doctors, are those who help people break addictions to medications and drugs of all kinds. The doctor who couldn't help me was a MAT doctor. I continued to use both because now I was really scared to stop knowing that stopping the benzodiazepines could potentially kill me. The pain pills withdrawals can't kill you although you may feel like you're dying when experiencing withdrawals from them. So, like with the pain pills, I started to taper myself down on the benzodiazepines. This battle would go on for the next few years.

One day, my boss from work called me and even though I was off on short term disability, I knew what she was calling me about. She had our human resources person on the phone as well and from previous experiences, I knew what this meant. I had been fired from every job because of using drugs and/or alcohol causing me to excessively miss work. When she told me, I wasn't even worried because when she called me, I was in the process of getting some pills and that's all I cared about at that moment.

Fifteen years and a lot of good memories gone down the drain and just like that, I was jobless for the first time in a long time. I told my fiancé right away, but I was once again too embarrassed to tell my family. I had great success working for that company and learned a lot along the way, so I decided to start my own business. I always loved to help people, so I based my business around helping small business owners like me, start, grow and thrive in the businesses. In the professional market this would be considered B2B, which is business to business.

I always prepared tax returns for myself, friends and family so I went on to get my license to prepare tax returns for my clients as well. This wasn't necessarily a B2B practice, but it still was a way for me to help people, so I incorporated this as a service offering by my business. I was still very much using pills but I would always make sure I had some so I could work effectively, and this got even more expensive. I was still making good money, but I was still spending it all on pills and bills.

By the time I was 44 years of age, things had only gotten worse with my addictions. I was facing a repossession of my vehicle, bills were months behind, and I was facing an eviction all at the same time. I'd decided to apply for help, through my local county, because they were providing financial assistance due to Covid. I was ten months behind on rent when they called me to let me know they paid all my back rent plus two months of future rent. I was so grateful of how things had worked out and I know this was another one of God's doing.

Any other circumstance and nowhere on the planet, would a landlord allow someone to go ten months without paying their rent. Even most family members would have evicted their loved ones after at least three months. I knew it was only a matter of time before they were going to be repossessing my vehicle, so I went out and got myself into more debt by buying a new car. I was not financially able to handle such a high car note exceeding nine hundred dollars monthly, not including insurance. It only took three months before they were looking to repossess the vehicle I'd recently purchased.

The other vehicle, I thought it was going to be repossessed but I had paid for all the principle and some interest, so I guess they decided to allow me to keep the vehicle. I now had two vehicles, and I was relieved I had a garage so I could keep my new vehicle hidden from the repo company. I would pay it up when I got money, and it would just fall behind again. This went on for two years until one day, unexpectedly, I was out and before I even left the place I was at, I could see out the window my car was gone, and I knew exactly why.

My oldest cousin came to visit me again. This was the same cousin who had come to stay with me in previous years, so he knew some of the people I knew and was familiar with the city. He knew I had a pill habit, but he didn't know how severe it was, but he was soon going to find out. He always told the family what was going on, almost like a spy, but I always appreciated his concern. Although it didn't feel good at the time of his doing, he would be the person to take the time and get me signed up for rehab, later, from a whole different city which was our hometown.

He was very observant and would make small remarks but he was very intelligent and older than me so there was nothing I could keep from him no matter how hard I tried. When I needed pills, no matter how humiliated I was, I would still find an excuse to get them even when someone was with me who I didn't want to know. It was like tunnel vision for me when I was on a mission to get pills.

On the day he left, he told me he knew what I was up to and that I needed to slow down because everywhere we went, I would stop first to get pills. He even called me on his way home to reiterate what he said before he left. Once he got back home, he let it be known to the family of what I was going through. They were all concerned, especially my mother. My mother always told me 'This too shall pass" and she was always right. My mother wasn't very affectionate, but she was always loyal and would be there for me whenever I needed her, no matter what. I still live by my mother's wise quotes to this very day.

Although my mother, fiancé and children knew what I was dealing with, they would still lend me money. My son, I always had to pay back with interest, my mother allowed me to not repay right away before she would lend me money again and my daughter never asked for the money back at all. I think they just didn't want to see me suffer because they all knew about my pill habit. I never told them how bad I felt when I didn't have any, but they could see my desperation for the pills.

45 years of age and hundreds of thousands of dollars over the years, gone due to my habits but the pull habit was the most expensive. I was now at the point where I compromised my dignity, self-respect and pride. I had never felt this low despite a life long of drugs and alcohol consumption. I started doing things I never imagined myself doing. Begging people for money, lying to my family and friends and allowing my immediate family to suffer as a result. This hurt my heart to know how bad I let them down. I always told them I was going to quit but because I was lying so much, they didn't believe me.

Deep down, I would think "is this really how my life is going to end"? I knew I was bigger than this habit, I just couldn't see a way to get from under it. Pills were by far a much worse habit because your body needs the pills, and you can function without them; NO ONE can. Medical providers must give you medication, which is derived from a common substance as the pills, as a form of treatment to stop using them. I was scared to try and get treatment because by law, you can't be prescribed pain pills while being treated to stop using pills. The medical providers also have access to see all the medications a person is being prescribed.

Due to this federal regulation in my country, a person can't even go to a different city or state to obtain pain pills if they are already being prescribed by any medical provider. There was also an epidemic, where people were selling fake pills and mixing fentanyl with pills and killing them instantly. This is the same cause of death of my son's father but it's still unclear if he knew he was ingesting fentanyl or not. Because of how bad a person feels when they don't have pills, I understood how a person would take anything out of desperation.

I was fortunate enough not to lose my life, but I did have one experience where I believe I ingested something other than a pill. Not sure if it was fentanyl but I was falling asleep mid-sentence while speaking to my fiancé, so I went to the emergency room. I didn't tell the doctor what I'd consumed, I just wanted to be in a hospital in case of an emergency. I ended up staying overnight until I knew the medication would be out of my system and no longer harmful.

The next morning when I was released from the hospital, I went to get more pills before I even went home. I didn't tell anyone what happened; not even my fiancé even though he was the one who'd taken me to the hospital. I knew if I had told him the truth, he would have been more concerned, so I made up a lie about the reason for my hospital visit.

I was just ready to get some more pills and if I were to tell him why I went to the hospital emergency room, because of pills, there was no way he would take me to get more, afterwards. A lot of serious things I kept hidden from my family and loved ones, because I didn't want to worsen their already negative thoughts about my pill habit. I didn't want to hear anyone's plea for me to stop so I would always tell them I had it under control, but I didn't, and they had no idea what I was going through internally nor the things I had done.

I was now 46 years of age and pretty much broke. No money, my family had also decided to stop lending me money. My mother still did but I hated to ask her. My business was failing, clients were displeased with my services and no matter hard I tried, things were falling apart – fast. I ended up doing the ultimate by using funds from my daughter's credit card, she allowed me to use to take care of personal business, and I betrayed her trust by misusing funds to support my pill habit.

Even though she forgave me, I was so disappointed in myself because now I wasn't only worrying about my family because of my habit; but I was now affecting their finances. She had to report her card stolen so it wouldn't affect her excellent credit, and I had the audacity to act as if I were mad because she reported her card stolen. We didn't speak for a few days after that, which felt like forever, because she and I had never gone through such a thing by not speaking to one another.

A few months prior she had just given fifteen hundred dollars to get my bills back on track, but I didn't use the money for bills, maybe the bare minimum, but the funds were used to support my pill habit. Over this time, I went from bank to bank ruining my accounts because I would constantly overdraft and couldn't afford to repay the money back. My credit was also in ruins due to my pill habit. I'd owed so many people and places it was ridiculous. I was also to the point of being sick of my own self. I couldn't trust or control myself. It was like someone else was inside of me making me make all these bad decisions and choices. I had ruined friendships but no matter what, my family still loved me.

My fiancé sat and watched me hit rock bottom. He pleaded with me, prayed for me and even cried about me. He couldn't believe who I had turned to. He was the closest person to me, so he witnessed everything. I would try and sneak to do things so we wouldn't argue about it but he would always know what I was up to. I even told him to leave me, but he just wouldn't and that's when I really knew, this man loves me with all his heart.

I kept promising him and my family I was going to get better, but at the time, those were just words with no actions. I still prayed each day and had a feeling; things weren't going to remain this way, but I just could not see how or a way out of this pill habit. I started thinking, maybe I really do need to lose everything and maybe that will make me snap out of it and while I did lose a lot, I never lost everything.

I stopped doing chores around the house, so my fiancé stepped up and started doing these things. He cooked, did all the household and grocery shopping and took care of the cleaning of our house inside and out. I kept thinking, "what would I do without him"? Through it all he was still being a good man to me, a good provider and overall, a good person. He started learning about the habit and now understood how serious it was. At first, he thought I was intentionally making the decisions I was making until he found out what strong hold pills can have on a person.

I was so busy living in the pill world I wasn't paying much attention to the real world and everything going on around me. I could not see things other people saw because I had one focus that would consume my energy and that would be pills. Getting pills is like a hi within itself, I always got excited knowing I was going to get some pills. At the time, that's all I looked forward to. Our household was in complete disarray. Although my fiancé took care of the household, he was still busy with his business and would sometimes work all day, coming home exhausted.

Before the pills, I never wanted to be away from him for more than a few hours, but now I would be happy when he wasn't around because then I could indulge in pills without him knowing. He still knew, he could tell if I needed some or had already had some. It got to the point where, when I would call him, it was to ask for money, so he now hated when I called him while he was working. When I wouldn't call him, he knew I would have pills. Our relationship went on like this for the next year straight.

I was now 47 years of age and when I first turned 47 years of age, I started to get serious about my sobriety. I allowed myself to suffer and was more disciplined with money. My support system was stronger than ever. It was a yearlong battle, but I also had no other medications to help me stop using pills, just support, the power of God and some all-natural supplements. It was a rocky road; I would stop completely for a couple of weeks and start back using pills again. I was also still being prescribed them, and my doctors had no idea about the struggles I was going through using the pills they were prescribing me.

As a matter of fact, I was now getting prescribed even more pills than ever before. Although my mother knew all about the bad habits, over the years, I never actually said the words to her or about anything I was going through because of abusing drugs. I would have to tell her about my troubled finances because she lent me money, but I would lie about the reason why I needed the money. I often wondered "why do these things keep happening to me' not realizing I had all the power to stop them already inside of me.

Things were spiraling despite me being serious about stopping using pills and things got worse before they got better. My daughter and oldest cousin took the time to get me signed up for rehab. I was excited to go but the rehab was anything but what I thought it would be. I felt worse than when I would be home withdrawing from using. They were giving me medication to prevent my being sick, but it didn't help with any other symptoms. I would always see documentaries or stories about rehab, and this was nothing like it I thought it would be.

I think it was because I was in an unfamiliar environment, didn't have access to my phone, family, or the outside world, or if I truly and mentally just wasn't prepared. I didn't want to attend group counseling meetings and would often just stay in my room. One morning the director came into my room and told me if I didn't participate, I would be kicked out.

I got checked in to rehab late at night. The drive was four hours from where I lived, and they picked me up at six p.m. Before I went, I took three different kinds of pills: pain pills, benzo's and sleeping pills. This was by far a deadly combination. I slept the whole ride there and was still sleeping in the lobby while waiting to be checked in. When they finally were ready to check me in, I woke up feeling hungover from pills.

Everybody had roommates but my roommate left the day after I came because when I arrived, she was sleep and I helped myself to one of her cigarettes since I wasn't allowed to have my vape while in there. She made a big deal about the situation, and I didn't want any trouble, I was feeling so bad being in there, I wasn't eating so I had no strength to deal with any drama even if I created the drama. It was a honest mistake and I explained to her, she was sleeping, and I didn't want to wake her.

    She didn't care; she was pissed. If we weren't in rehab, which is a place of peace, she probably would have tried to fight me, and I was completely defenseless. She moved to another room, and I was happy to be in the room alone. The staff confronted me about the situation and that was only my first day there and I had already caused all of this.

    I had replaced smoking cigarettes with vaping ten years prior but when I didn't have a vape, I would resort back to smoking. Not for long but just enough time, in between, until I got another vape. It's still a bad habit just without smoke but now I'm not sure what other health risks vape's carry which could be potentially worse than smoking cigarettes. I also used to think cigarette habits cost more, over time, than vaping but it really depends on how often a person uses their vape to determine.

    It was only a seventy-two-hour detox so I was looking forward to leaving so I could get back home and get some pills. My prescribing doctors still didn't know any of what was going on. I met some nice people, however, and they were in great spirits so I would go around them when I came out of my room. Although it was only seventy-two hours, it felt way longer. Finally, they told me when I would be leaving, and I was happy. In my exit counseling meeting I met a Chaplin, who had been addicted to heroin for over twenty years and now clean for fifteen years and he prayed with me. After he prayed, he told me he had a good feeling about me and said I was going to be alright and despite how bad I was feeling from the withdrawals; I never let those words go.

They couldn't bring me back to my home, which is where they picked me up from, so they dropped me off at a local sober living home, which I told them immediately I was not staying and called my fiancé to come get me. My fiancé then called my daughter and oldest cousin, who had taken their time to get me admitted to the rehab and were proud of me for going, and they both called me and asked me why I was leaving. They were both disappointed in me, but they quickly got over it. My fiancé picked me up and the first thing I told him was that I was going to get pills.

He was pissed, I made excuses of why I left, and I didn't regret leaving. That rehab truly was not a good fit for me. I felt like I needed to be home because I needed to make money, and I couldn't make money being in rehab. Sure, there are people who work while in rehab, but I could not run my business from rehab and getting a job was not an option for me. The coordinator of the sober living home briefly spoke to me before he had to go into a meeting and asked me to wait but as soon as my fiancé got there, I left without evening signing my release forms. I knew I was closer to getting pills and I never let anything, or anyone get in the way of that.

Once I got home and got some pills I still didn't feel better immediately. It took a couple of days before I felt normal again, because I now had pills, but I couldn't help thinking whatever medication they gave me had an unpleasant lasting effect. I'm sure it was for the good, but I didn't stick around long enough to find out. It was also the first time I felt like that during a withdrawal period. It was like the medication they had given me didn't allow the pills to work.

Things started to take a dip again, and finally I was truly done with pain pills. On Thanksgiving, which I am thankful for, I couldn't get any pills, and I was forced to confront this habit that haunted me the last seven years of my life. When I faced it headfirst it was like I had removed some foggy glasses I'd been wearing. I could now see why I went through everything I went through and survived it all - But God! I was finally releasing the tight grip I had on pills and the thought of being afraid of how I would feel. My pill habit was gone, and I don't mean like it's a struggle everyday and I can't be around drugs… ALL my bad habits that ran my life for years are gone. I was reborn.

I felt the addiction leave my body and I told my family, but I had been telling them for years I was going to stop or had already stopped so I don't think they really believed me at first. The first couple of weeks, they started to notice. My problematic finances, which were a result of my pill addictions, were still there but I was still relieved the habit was gone because I knew I could now fix my finance problems by saving a lot of money. I had a stack of mail I finally decided to go through and there were not one, but two checks made out to me.

I had not been expecting this money and if I had been to see those checks just two weeks earlier, which was how long they had been there, I would have spent the money on pills. This experience further confirmed that I was free of my habits. I was too busy chasing pills and would let my mail pile up and I am so thankful I did this time. I felt great, greater than I had felt since I was thirteen years of age. For this first time in my life, since I was thirteen years of age I had been abusing substances of all kinds. I am now 47 years of age and completely sober.

This led me to go on a spiritual journey because I had to become familiar with myself. My spiritual journey then led me closer to God, which I'd always prayed and talked to God but for real, now. I'm not a holly roller but I constantly thank God and meditate daily. I am living proof and here to tell anyone who is going through something similar, you are more powerful than you know if you just believe, trust the process and trust God!

Explore and learn more about published authors affiliated with KLE.

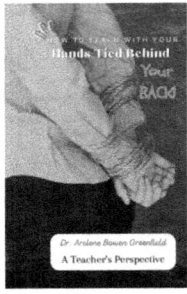    

KLEPub.com

SCAN ME

Call or Text:
770-240-0089 Press Extension 1
Web: KLEpub.com
Email Services@klepub.com

It's time to start and finish   **YOUR Story!**

KLE Publishing specializes in helping people become authors. In as little as 15 to 90 days, we can help you develop your books and e-books and publish to 39,000 outlets! We also offer audiobook services.

Write, Edit, Format, Publish
We can help from
Start to Finish.